This Poison Called Depression

Larry E. Van Essen

Inspiring Voices®
A Service of **Guideposts**

Copyright © 2013 Larry E. Van Essen.

All rights reserved. No part of this book may be used or reproduced by any means, graphic, electronic, or mechanical, including photocopying, recording, taping or by any information storage retrieval system without the written permission of the publisher except in the case of brief quotations embodied in critical articles and reviews.

Inspiring Voices books may be ordered through booksellers or by contacting:

Inspiring Voices
1663 Liberty Drive
Bloomington, IN 47403
www.inspiringvoices.com
1-(866) 697-5313

Because of the dynamic nature of the Internet, any web addresses or links contained in this book may have changed since publication and may no longer be valid. The views expressed in this work are solely those of the author and do not necessarily reflect the views of the publisher, and the publisher hereby disclaims any responsibility for them.

Any people depicted in stock imagery provided by Thinkstock are models, and such images are being used for illustrative purposes only. Certain stock imagery © Thinkstock.

All scripture quotations are from NIV Study Bible Zondervan Publishing House, Grand Rapids, Michigan, 10th Anniversary Edition, Copyright 1995

ISBN: 978-1-4624-0586-2 (sc)

Printed in the United States of America.

Inspiring Voices rev. date: 4/23/2013

With deep gratitude
To
God

For the encouragement and support
of my family and friends

My daughters: Becky Te Velde, Leah
Geertsema, Sarah Willborn
And their husbands: Bernard, Mark and Casey
And our grandchildren: Fred and Kelsey,
Adam, Jake, Lauren, Alex, Jaclyn, Simon,
Jordan, Michaela, Sean, Isaac and Ethan

And, most importantly,
My wife Betty

Table of Contents

Foreword ix

Introduction. 1

Chapter 1: The anatomy of a depression 7

Chapter 2: The timeline of a depression 21

Chapter 3: The effects of depression 27

Chapter 4: The role of Scripture, prayer, worship and caregivers in the healing of depression. 47

Chapter 5: The role of medication in the treatment of major depression 55

Chapter 6: The role of a therapist in the treatment of major depression 59

Chapter 7: The providence of God in depression . . .63

Chapter 8: Relapses 71

Epilogue. 75

About the Author. 79

Bibliography. 81

Foreword

Uninvited, depression came in, sat right down at Larry Van Essen's dinner table thirty years ago, and off and on, without warning or permission, took over the central conversation of his marriage and ministry, of his life.

Now recovered, with the darker experiences of his mental illness behind him and plenty of sunny days in his life, Larry has done us a big favor describing in candid detail the illness that disabled his closest relationships, sapped his drive for ministry, and sucked the fun out of life. And Larry shares important information about depression that he discovered along the way.

A life-friend and colleague, I know Larry could have written authentically about other, happier ministry experiences – loving neighbors with Betty, his wife, into the Kingdom, effective gospel preaching, about leading growing congregations.

But I'm glad he wrote "This Poison Called Depression". There is just is not much out there written by a minister who has suffered it. His book offers help for ministers, church workers, and ministry leaders like me who relate to others with depression, yet have a hard time speaking of one's own. (I estimate at least half of us in ministry leadership, including me, have experienced depression in some form that depreciates close relationships, ministry, joy.)

Thanks, Larry! For the hard work of writing as you have. Reading "This Poison Called Depression" blessed and benefited me; I recommend it.

John Rozeboom
A pastor of Oakdale Park Church, Grand Rapids, Mich.,
Director Emeritus/Christian Reformed Home Missions
Grand Rapids, Michigan
April 12, 2013

Introduction

I was sitting in study hall in high school and there was a knock on the door. The teacher in charge went to the door and then he came to me. "Your brother is in the hall and would like to talk to you." I went out to my brother, Howard, and he said: "Dad and someone else had to take Mom to Grand Rapids, Michigan, where she can receive treatment for a nervous breakdown. You can ride home as you normally do and we'll go from there." After he left I thought, "Nervous breakdown? What in the world is that?" As I thought about it, I began to speculate that maybe some of the "unusual" behavior of Mom lately was related to this breakdown. She could hardly vacuum the carpet, wash our clothes, cook, or polish the floors. She complained about being exhausted most of the time.

Later that day, my basketball coach approached me and said, "Larry I heard about your mom going to the hospital today. If you would rather not play tonight that is ok with me, you do not have to. But I'll leave the choice to you." I said, "I do not know what else I would do if I did not play so I would prefer to play." I played one of the best games of my life. I had twelve points by halftime, but did not score a point the second half.

This event was an early indication that this "breakdown" could affect my life in unusual ways. As the years passed the word "breakdown" was no longer used to describe what mom had. Instead the words major depression or clinical depression came into use. In those days, little did I know that what mom was experiencing would become one of my major challenges as well.

"At the most unexpected moments it slips people its dark poison. One scarcely notices the initial sting. Slowly, insidiously, the poison spreads until the victim finds herself cut off from life by a gray veil. The monster, what Winston Churchill, a longtime sufferer called the 'Black Dog,' is depression" (Timmerman 213).

Since I turned 40 in February of 1984, I have had eight episodes of major depression. By episode, I mean a period of time ranging from 6–24 weeks of clinical (major) depression as diagnosed by a psychiatrist. One episode, the last to this point, lasted for 18 months. Each episode has consisted of feelings of being overwhelmed, high anxiety, worthlessness, emptiness, hopelessness, incompetence, joylessness, lack of clarity and ability to concentrate. All of these feelings and characteristics are in direct contradiction to much of what one's life in Christ can be. We are promised as Christians by our Lord: "I have come that they may have life, and have it to the full" (John 10:10). "Fullness of Life" seems non-existent when one is depressed.

When we think of the first and greatest commandment, we are reminded that it centers in love. We are to love God, love our neighbor and love ourselves.

Introduction discussion questions

1. Have you or any family member experienced major depression? Can you describe for the group what that was like?

2. Why is Timmerman's description of major depression as being 'cut off from life by a gray veil" a good or poor description of major depression?

3. What would you say are the major signs of major depression?

4. How can a depressed person best deal with the gap between what the Bible teaches regarding the Christian life and what is in fact their experience at the moment?

5. Do you think that 30 people in your church are currently taking anti-depressants?

Chapter I

The anatomy of a depression

When I awoke on October 6, 2006, it was a morning like any other. We had just returned home from a two week trip to the Midwest to visit children, siblings and take in the wedding of my wife Betty's nephew. All seemed well, although I had said to Betty "I think I am getting depressed, but I do not know what to do about it." I naively hoped that I was ready to resume my work as Pastor of Congregational Life and Outreach at Visalia Christian Reformed Church. It was Thursday. The only thing I had that was pressing was a wedding on Saturday. Being part of a staff ministry and not being the senior pastor meant that I was not scheduled to preach on Sunday. This I thought would be a relaxing weekend punctuated with the joy of an especially heartwarming wedding of two believers in Jesus Christ. But Thursday and Friday went by with a sluggish kind of pace and I had a feeling that something was not right. Just what, I did not know or did not want to know. You see, what I was going to find out very soon was that I had slipped back into a seventh depression. Perhaps I was just in denial, or the cursed feelings of depression had not yet totally hit me. By Saturday they had. Although I was playing a minor role, the wedding details already in the morning were beginning to overwhelm me as if I had never officiated at a wedding before in my life. I had been a pastor for 37 years and the number of weddings at which I had officiated was substantial—so to feel this threatened and nervous was not normal for me.

I gradually had to admit the old "dark cloud" that Abraham Lincoln used to talk about had come back. I have come to hate it when I have to admit to myself, to Betty, the family, and to those close to me that I'm depressed. I mean clinically depressed. I'm not talking about having a bad hair day, or having the blues, or suffering from some anxiety associated with a particular event that has happened or is about to happen. No, I'm talking about complete dis-ease. Dis-ease with oneself, dis-ease with all one's relationships, dis-ease with life, and dis-ease with God. I'm talking about what William Styron described as the indescribable:

> If the pain were readily describable most of the countless sufferers from this ancient affliction would have been able to confidently depict for their friends and loved ones (even their physicians) some of the actual dimensions of their torment, and perhaps elicit a comprehension that has been generally lacking; such incomprehension has usually been due not to failure of sympathy

This Poison Called Depression

but to the basic inability of healthy people to imagine a form of torment so alien to everyday experience. (17)

Depression is never easy. It is an ugly time for the afflicted and for all the significant others affected. Lillian Grissen aptly writes: "The depressed person does not live at the bottom of the sea; he lies beneath the bottom" (202). When I hear about people who take their own lives because they were depressed, it does not surprise me but it deeply saddens me. How is it possible that in a day when we can communicate with gadgets in outer space, we still cannot figure out something to prevent these troubled souls from taking matters into their own hands? In a world where we all walk around with cell phones by which we can call or text each other, find out the latest news, weather, sports, and get directions to a store's location, how is it possible for a young mother of five to become so despondent that she drowns her own children in her bathtub? How is it possible that a depressed person, as happened in our town, shot and killed a much loved Mormon bishop? How can a depressed person in Aurora, Colorado, go to a theater and open fire on a crowd, killing twelve and wounding many more? Astonishingly, as I am writing these words, the news is filled with the tragic account of a shooting in a Newtown, CT. elementary school taking the lives of 20 children and 7 adults. The shooter also took his own life. Again much speculation is taking place regarding the mental health of the shooter and the appropriate role of guns in our society.

Yes, depression is indescribable. In an article in *Christianity Today*, Christine A. Scheller quotes Kay Redfield Jamison, Johns Hopkins University professor of psychiatry in an attempt to describe the indescribable:

> From the time I woke up in the morning until the time I went to bed at night, I was unbearably miserable and seemingly incapable of any kind of joy or enthusiasm. Everything—every thought, word, movement—was an effort. Everything that once was sparkling was now flat. . . . The wretched, convoluted, and pathetically confused mass of gray worked only well enough to torment me with a dreary litany of my inadequacies and shortcomings in character, and to taunt me with the total, desperate hopelessness of it all. . . . Death and its kin were constant companions. (40)

My first personal brush with depression came in Riverside, California. In the same year that I turned 40, 1984, I became totally lethargic, unable to concentrate, felt worthless, incompetent, and struggled mightily to get my pastoral responsibilities done. I thought it would fade away but it continued for several months. I spoke with a hospital chaplain, (whom I had met along the way) at Voorman's Psychiatric Medical Center about my situation and he arranged for me to meet with a psychiatrist.

The psychiatrist asked me a number of questions: "What do you do for pleasure?" "Any hobbies, outside of ministry interests?"

This Poison Called Depression

I could not think of anything.

"How is your marriage, family life, ministry life? Anything stressing you out there?"

I could not think of anything.

"Well," he said, "you are obviously very angry with someone."

I could not think of anyone.

"You are angry with yourself."

"I am not aware of being angry with myself," I said.

"You are beating up on yourself," came the all too quick response.

"You are telling yourself that you are no good, worthless, incompetent, and a piece of s_____." That got a little closer to home than I was prepared for and I had to admit that I did not think very well of myself. He said, "You have to get your own cup filled first. You cannot minister to others, if you do not have anything in your cup to minister from." That made sense. Thankfully my time was up. That was enough for one hour. We parted with him saying, "You do not need to see me again unless you want to. You can find any number of good psychiatrists right there in Riverside, if you want to." I went home with plenty of meat to chew on. But I did nothing except to tell Betty about it, and she right away thought that the idea of filling my own cup was right on target. I thought about it but started feeling better so never went any farther with filling my cup.

Unfortunately, about a year later, the same thing came back, only this time more intense. So I went to a psychologist in Riverside who talked with me and gave me a test. His observations were very similar to the first doctor I saw. He also thought I could benefit from the reading of John Bradshaw's book *On the Family*. Bradshaw's book had by this time become a highly regarded book on the nature of functional and dysfunctional families. He said he wanted me to see a psychiatrist to determine if I needed to be on medication. I did and the psychiatrist's conclusion was that in addition to medication I should make filling my own life with good things a much higher priority. This was the beginning of a long journey which I am still on today.

Depression is baffling. To the concerned family member or friend, sometimes even therapists, depression appears to be something about which one can do something. This may be true in some situations. It certainly is not true when the cause comes from within the person. Archibald Hart explains in his book *Dark Clouds–Silver Linings* that, broadly speaking, there are three major categories of depression. I find these distinctions helpful in understanding depression. "First, there are endogenous depressions. These come from within the body. They are generally understood to be caused by biochemical disturbances in the brain, the hormonal system, or the nervous system. Some are the direct cause of disease or infection." (2) In a different book, *Counseling the Depressed*, Dr. Hart cites a "Special Report on Depression Research" from the National Institute of Mental Health:

> This report emphasizes that at a fundamental level, all behavioral responses to our world are dependent on electrical and neurochemical

transmission in the brain. Nerve impulses trigger the release of neurotransmitters, or special chemical messengers. Every nerve pathway has special synapses and the purpose of the neurotransmitter is to help the nerve signal jump across this gap" (90).

This is the kind of depression I primarily experienced and am describing. Because of endogenous causes, depressed people often speak about a dullness of mind or a frozen brain without an ability to focus or concentrate. It is a brain that is largely out of control. What one can do easily normally, suddenly becomes a mountainous and gigantic task. I could stand at the closet for five minutes trying to decide what to wear. While this may be normal for some, believe me, it does not normally take this long for me. Dr. Hart continues:

> The second group of depressions is known as exogenous depressions [meaning "from without"]. These are reactions to what is going on externally, the depressions we experience in day-to-day living. They are psychological in nature. . . .
>
> The third group of depressions I call the neurotic depressions. These differ from reactive depressions in that they're responses to the stresses and anxieties of life that have built up over a long period. They happen when we don't grieve our losses in a healthy way. (*Counseling the Depressed* 2–3)

Larry E. Van Essen

In *Dark Clouds; Silver Linings*, Hart adds the following regarding endogenous depression: "We don't fully understand everything about how the brains chemistry can be disturbed, but these depressions respond so well to antidepressant medication that it is generally accepted that that they have a biochemical basis." (2) If a depression can have a biochemical basis, then it becomes clear to me that it is not helpful to say to a depressed person, "you should exercise more regularly, read your Bible more faithfully, pray more fervently, stop dwelling on your depression, think more positively, and take the focus off of yourself, and then, perhaps, the Lord would bring you victory." This does not mean that any one of these alone or all of them together could not help anyone at anytime in their life. But to focus on self-help exercises alone for a biologically based depression is simply devaluing the suffering that is taking place. It is cruel and flows from ignorance regarding depression. I can assure you it is not the best way to win the friendship of depressed people. They resent it and well they should. Imagine saying to a person suffering with cancer: "forget taking those chemical treatments or radiation treatments, if you would just adopt a positive attitude or eliminate certain negative and self-defeating thinking patterns you would get better." Yet unfortunately things like this are said to people with depression. Not because of malice but of misunderstanding

Clinically depressed people are not able to get themselves out of their depression. And this may be baffling to those who come alongside of the depressed

This Poison Called Depression

person. Why can you not just snap out of it? Why can you not just make one right decision and then another and another and gradually simply walk out of your pit? Indeed this "advice" baffles depressed people and increases their pain. They feel like they should be able to get out of their depression. They ask: if everybody else can why can't I? This begins a cycle of guilt and shame.

Since I am not getting better, I must not be trying hard enough, and if I am not trying hard enough, I am lazy. And if I am lazy, that makes me guilty of sin. And if I am guilty of sin and cannot get well, that must mean I am not confessing my sin properly before God, or perhaps I may have sinned beyond the bounds of his grace, perhaps like Judas. One can become increasingly convinced that she has committed the unpardonable sin against the Holy Spirit. My mother often struggled with this thought. This cycle of inability, guilt and shame, worthlessness and hopelessness can, if not carefully treated and monitored, lead to suicide. I know from experience that it is only the gentle but firm hands of God that have held me back. Only his faithfulness and unconditional love saved me from doing what others have done. I can only believe that God in his grace and justice will deal with them in a gracious and just manner. Gracious because God will deal with them in light of his gift of eternal life for all sinners who believe in Jesus; just because God will deal with them as he does with all Christians in light of having judged or punished our sins when Jesus died on the cross for our sins. "He did it to demonstrate his justice at the present time, so as to be just and the one who justifies those who have faith in Jesus" (Romans 3: 26).

One weekend I was feeling horrible. I was saying scary things and thinking even scarier things like "I do not know why I'm still alive." "I'm not getting any better." "It seems like my best way out of this predicament is death." I was desperate and hopeless. I could not appreciate reminders that I had a wonderful wife, family, friends and otherwise good health. It seemed best to Betty and the family that I should be hospitalized. Betty and Pastor Vink took me to the emergency room. I cannot remember very well what all took place in the emergency room. Someone gave me a shot and stuffed me in what seemed to me like a chamber in which I would slide back and forth. I thought they were going to kill me. I have asked Betty about this contraption, but she has no idea what I am talking about. Perhaps this was a product of hallucination. After consultation with a social worker, Betty, and my daughter, I was transferred to a mental hospital in Fresno. Never in my wildest dreams, did I expect to end up in a mental hospital. I knew that my mother had gone to Pine Rest Christian Hospital in Grand Rapids, Michigan, several times in her life, but I never thought that I would hear the door slam behind and realize that I was prisoner. It was frightening to me but also emotionally draining for Betty and our children.

In the Fresno hospital, I received numerous visits by a variety of physicians, social workers, and counselors. My medicine prescriptions were changed several times and I felt somewhat better. The hospital could only keep

This Poison Called Depression

me for 72 hours and then if I wanted more care I could voluntarily commit myself. One counselor said, "You need to find a new way of handling stress," implying, I thought, that my problem was a simple matter of proper skills and that some kind of behavioral change could make me better. Such an understanding, I think, completely oversimplifies what depression is, particularly one with a biological component. One psychologist came in and started berating us for being in a mental hospital. Perhaps he thought we *wanted* to be there. In his speech he argued against the use of medication for depression because, he said, drugs are ineffective. He described us as the clowns, black sheep, and morons in our family. I had never thought of myself in those terms. I started talking to some other patients to see what they thought of him, but they did not want to say much. One said, "You had better be careful or you will be in here for a long time." Being a preacher, I knew the trouble you could get into by saying the wrong thing. I thought the psychologist was guilty of verbal abuse. But was I in any kind of condition to make that judgment? After three days, they said I could go home. I remember that Betty was very uncomfortable with me coming home, but I was unwilling to commit myself to further treatment. Now as I look back I wonder why I did not use this opportunity for greater treatment? Was it concern for the cost? Was it the stigma of being in a mental hospital? Did I actually think that I could go home and with outpatient professional care I would get well?

I had several visits from pastors of the church and

friends. They were much appreciated. I remember a meeting of Betty, Becky, and Sarah (my wife and two daughters) and me with a psychologist. But I cannot remember specifically what was said or planned.

The first couple of days at home went okay. Towards the end of the week, I was having serious problems with the regular symptoms of depression. I think it was Thursday night that Betty asked Rev. Herm Minnema to come over to talk with me. He did, and everything he said made sense and was supportive, but I was not feeling any better. I truly appreciated his time and presence with me and his prayer. By Friday I called 911. The operator asked if I thought I might do myself harm, to which I said I really did not know. A police officer came to the door and wanted to talk with me. He asked how I was feeling and other questions to see if I could be at home or if I needed to go to the hospital again. I thought I would be okay. So he left. My neighbor also came over to check and I told her I would be okay. But my feelings started to get more intense. It was not long and a police car, an ambulance, and a fire truck were parked in front of the house. A police officer came in the house and ushered me to his car. Off to Kaweah Hospital I went again. After that initial procedure, which I cannot figure out to this day, I was transferred to our local Kaweah Delta Mental Hospital. Since it was the weekend, very little in the area of therapy occurred. I remember walking down the hall thinking that all the people I met were in a ghost like dimension. I would talk to them but I could not tell if they were real. It was horrible. A social worker took me

This Poison Called Depression

aside and I asked, "What is going on with me?" He said, "You were hallucinating." I never want to do that again.

This time Betty asked the staff to recommend a psychiatrist. They suggested one. He felt I was completely over-medicated and that some medications were actually fighting with each other. He changed the medical package. This time we also decided to stay for two weeks and at the end of that time I started to feel somewhat better. During this hospitalization, I had visits from the family and fellow church members. During all my episodes of depression, I had tremendous family support and that of friends. They were always an integral part of my healing. Pastor Vink also stopped by. He had seen me many times throughout this whole episode, because of our mutual ministry at church, and had assured me that nothing could separate me from the love of God in Christ Jesus. He repeated it: "Nothing." I am thankful for his non-judgmental support. Again it was time to go home but this time I gradually became better so that I went back to work at church almost immediately.

On reflection, this was way too soon. I felt good and actually started a new church program called Celebrate Recovery in the fall of 2006. But gradually the symptoms of depression were coming back. I was completely frustrated. I had to drop out of Celebrate Recovery, which made me sad for the volunteers and for this program that was showing a great deal of potential.

Chapter 1 discussion questions

1. What is there about depression that makes it very hard for the afflicted to describe it to others? Does this make sense to you?

2. How does filling ones cup relate to depression? Could it prevent it, reduce it, or eradicate it?

3. Do the distinctions made between depressions help you understand what is going on in these different types of depression?

4. Why are various self-help exercises limited in their effectiveness for biological depression?

Chapter 2

The timeline of a depression

When I consider the timeline for depression in my life, I have to go back to my mother whom I know suffered serious episodes of depression and three distinct times had to be hospitalized at Pine Rest. Pine Rest was a Christian Hospital in Grand Rapids, Michigan, where one could receive treatment for what we then referred to as a "nervous breakdown." Today we call it clinical or major depression. Mom had to stay there for about 8 weeks and then was able to come home and did very well for most of the time. But this old black cloud would come back to her over the years, off and on. Her times in between episodes would be very good. I knew she was having a tough mental time because she would sometimes talk to me about how she felt. She would say, "I do not know what is wrong with me, but I just lack energy to do anything." "I feel so empty inside". "I must have done something wrong because God is allowing this to happen to me." Once she said she thought she had committed the

Larry E. Van Essen

unpardonable sin. I tried to reason with her, but at age 16, I did not realize that her mind was not functioning right. I remember reading to her from Hebrews 12 about how God disciplines those he loves. To me verses 10-11 were very encouraging: "Our fathers disciplined us for a little while as they thought best; but God disciplines us for our good, that we may share in his holiness. No discipline seems pleasant at the time, but painful. Later on, however, it produces a harvest of righteousness and peace for those who have been trained by it." I thought perhaps she would be encouraged by the thought that God understood that her sickness was painful but later it would produce a harvest of righteousness and peace. I do not think my efforts helped her very much. All we could do now was pray that God would use Pine Rest to bring her back to health. Once I asked my psychiatrist, "Why has another episode of depression touched me?" He simply responded, "It's in the genes." I wish it were not so but I think he is right, partially right for sure. It seems to fit my experience. It is noteworthy that to the best of my knowledge my three siblings and three daughters have not had major depression for which I am grateful.

Usually I cannot pinpoint a trigger nor can I point to any one thing that brings me out of it other than medication, rest, prayer and support from family members and friends. So my depression timeline goes back nearly 60 years, since my mother had her first bout with depression shortly after I was born and she turned 40. Interestingly, my first episode also began when I turned 40. My first depressions did not last nearly as long as my last two depressions (2001) and (2005-07). The first ones lasted between 6 to 8 weeks, but they steadily increased to 12–14 weeks and culminated with my last one taking nearly 1½ years. In 1997 in Madison, Wisconsin, I had to take a three month leave of absence from my work as Pastor of Crossroads Church, a Ministry of the Christian Reformed Church. I simply was unable to handle even the most routine pastoral responsibilities. How could that be so? I was doing what I earnestly believed God had called me do, and I was doing what I enjoyed doing except for this horrible depression thing. I sometimes would call Betty at her work and tell her that she had to come home. Thankfully she had an understanding boss who would let her come home and then return later. My psychiatrist has told me that, generally speaking, each additional episode takes longer to overcome and is more difficult to treat. Again this fits my experience. Lillian Grissen makes the following observation: "With depression one cannot look back a week or a day and expect to see progress. One has to ask, 'Am I better today than I was a month ago? Three months ago? A year ago?'" (93)

I mention the duration of the depression simply because depressed persons sometimes get so discouraged that they stop taking their medication, thinking that it is not working anyway, or they try to do harm to themselves in desperation. Perhaps if they knew that this is not unusual they would be able to place their illness in a more realistic context. Sometimes my psychiatrists would suggest that in three or four weeks I should start noticing the difference. Rarely did it happen that fast. I would encourage the depressed person and family to be patient, very patient, patient like they may have never been before. In due time, the recovery will come, in God's time. Please do not lose heart. William Styron observes, "Even those for whom any kind of therapy is a futile exercise can look forward to the eventual passing of the storm. If they survive the storm itself, its fury almost always fades and then disappears. Mysterious in its coming, mysterious in its going, the affliction runs its course, and one finds peace" (73).

The episode can turn around very suddenly as it did with me in 2006. For nearly 1½ years I was depressed, experiencing high anxiety at certain times of the day. Often I thought that the high anxiety was worse than the depression. I was losing hope. Then my doctor asked me if I had ever used a medication to treat my high anxiety that had been somewhat effective, and I said I had; it was clonazepam (klonopin). He remarked that it was a rather old medication and that he would try it starting that evening. The next day I felt no anxiety, nor the next, nor the days since. In one day with the right medication my episode was over! I can only thank God for turning my affliction into joy. I say joy because when the cloud of depression lifts it is like you are reborn. All is alive and well. The trees clap their hands.

Chapter 2 discussion questions

1. Do you think that some kinds of depression are genetic?

2. Why is it often ineffective to reason with or read scripture to depressed people?

3. What does Styron mean when he says: "Even those for whom any kind of therapy is a futile exercise can look forward to the eventual passing of the storm."?

4. Is there a definite timeline for major depression?

Chapter 3

The effects of depression

The effects of depression are mentally shattering, life threatening, and relationally hurtful. They are shattering when it comes to one's concept of self. Depression hammers home the lie that one is worthless, incompetent, and unforgiveable with a barrage of hopeless and self-condemning thoughts. The damage to one's self-image is perhaps the most heinous of its effects. I have never spoken to a single person who has experienced clinical depression for whom one or more of these symptoms were not true. The words of some of the Psalms, like 42:5, capture the power of this disease when they say: "Why are you downcast, O my soul? Why so disturbed within me?" The question of the psalmist goes unanswered in my mind to this day. My life for sixty-plus years has been enjoyable, productive, and meaningful. But when depression comes, I live under the bottom.

My depression is there like a lightning bolt or perhaps like the sting of a bee and I ponder the question: "Why are you downcast, O my soul?" This becomes painful when bystanders and therapists suggest that it generally is due to stress or anger and that one simply needs to adjust one's skills or attitude to overcome it. A variety of human activities can be put into practice, sometimes they can help many people, but they are not the silver bullet for clinical depression (endogenous), at least in my experience. They are nothing but band aids for a hemorrhaging blood vessel. Often such suggestions simply add to the pain and loneliness.

In addition, I often experienced a brain that simply did not function properly. It refused to focus or concentrate sufficiently to meet the demands of work or whatever I wanted to do. Strangely, simultaneously the brain gives the message that one is incompetent and brain frozen and at the same time raises the level of expectations so high that a double-whammy occurs. On the one hand, one is incompetent and on the other hand one must perform at nearly perfectionist standards. This of course leads to frustration. The feelings of incompetence strongly suggest that one had best take less risk and have less exposure to error. The answer seems to be a cutback in one's schedule. Often this is a needed response because it allows for some badly needed rest, but it has its downside. The downside is that as one reduces her schedule one's sense of incompetence can intensify. All one needs at such a time is a mistake that is noticed by others and brought to one's attention to make the case that certainly one is worthless and incompetent.

I cannot speak for others but what became the most

This Poison Called Depression

debilitating factor in my last depression was the conviction and lie that I was unforgiveable. It is most sobering that this occurred not when I was an immature Christian but after nearly forty-five years of walking with Jesus. Depression shows no mercy.

I had taken a walk in which I was silently talking to God. I thought I heard him say, "You need to stop haranguing Betty about your illness." I said, "I will." When I came in the house, I promptly went to Betty and began to tell her how awful I felt. I broke my promise to God within five minutes. Again I thought I heard God say: "Okay, that's it. Now you have gone too far." Why a mental health issue should carry such a powerful spiritual bombshell I do not begin to understand. All I know is that depression with its feelings of "never will I know forgiveness" has its origin in the deepest part of the pit of outer darkness where there will be weeping and gnashing of teeth.

Satan is indeed a liar, and a murderer, and a robber. All that is precious in the Christian faith: the comfort and joy of salvation, the presence of the Holy Spirit, the assurance of being a child of God, and any sense of growing into the likeness of Christ gets challenged, almost snuffed out, by **this poison called DEPRESSION**. The comfort of Psalm 139:7–10 "Where can I go from your Spirit? Where can I flee from your presence? If I go to the heavens, you are there; if I make my bed in the depths you are there. If I rise on the wings of the dawn, if I settle on the far side of the sea, even there your hand will guide me and right hand will hold me fast," rolled off my soul like so much water off a duck's back. It simply could not penetrate my heart. If it did, it was discomforting because this meant that God knew everything about me, and I was convinced that he could/would not find anything good.

Depression, as I have already suggested, is also life-threatening. This I believe is a truth that is taken far too lightly in society and in the church. The statistics of people with depression who commit suicide are very high. Dr. Hart writes, "Researchers estimate that between 30 and 70 percent of suicides are completed by people diagnosed as having major depression and 15 percent of people with major depression commit suicide. In my experience, I have never known anyone to commit suicide who hasn't been depressed" (*Counseling* 232). Why this does not prompt us who are caring for depressed people to be very cautious about leaving them alone is amazing. I understand it because we all have jobs, things to do, and are very busy. But it is very common that the depressed person in the privacy of his or her car, home, or some other secluded area commits suicide. When one feels to the core that he or she is unforgiveable and unredeemable, suicide seems like a logical and attractive choice. It may even feel like it is one's duty to rid one's family and world of such a trouble maker. One is not toying with his salvation, since he is already convinced he is headed for condemnation. Please remember, I am not saying that this is actually the case, but rather that is how I felt and this was my faulty perception of reality.

Today almost all of us in the church have had a relative, friend, or acquaintance who committed suicide. It is

This Poison Called Depression

morally imperative, that we come to a better understanding in our communities and churches of our responsibility to depressed persons and their families. When I was in my teens, three fellow Christians of the same church denomination committed suicide in the same year. I remember no formal effort to investigate the reason(s) for this, although I cannot recall another time or place where this occurred. One would think that such an unlikely occurrence would prompt some kind of study. When I was at Dordt College, a classmate, perhaps the brightest in the class, committed suicide. As I recall, nothing much was said about this baffling tragedy. I am aware of a man with mental issues who killed a Mormon bishop in the past year. I am also aware of the man in Tucson, Arizona, with mental issues who shot congresswoman Giffords, killed six, and injured twelve others. In this latter incident I feel that his outbursts at school, students being afraid of him, and his suspension from college were signals that he was not healthy. He needed protection, safety, and treatment. And the public deserved safety. I have been very impressed by Congressman Jesse Jackson Jr. who admitted himself to Mayo Clinic to treat a bipolar mental condition. That had to be a very difficult decision given the stigma still attached to mental illness and what consequences it might have on his political career. Astonishingly as I write these words another horrific tragedy has occurred. A twenty year old man entered a Newtown, Connecticut elementary school shooting 20 children and six adults. Prior to this attack he had shot and killed his mother. There are again a number of actions being considered.

Larry E. Van Essen

A ban on assault weapons, back ground checks for all who buy guns, registration of all people who own and purchase guns, study of mental health procedures, and the role that evil plays in these incidents. The Christian faith has long held to a teaching, the sinful nature of all people, which I think gives us strong theological guidance on this issue. When we talk about persons with mental health issues we need to discard all pejorative labeling of such people as "the crazies", "maniacs, and "the idiots". I have heard these words used in describing the people who have committed these crimes on T.V., in newspaper articles and especially talk radio. The persons who make these statements appear to be completely blind to their own sinful thoughts and behavior. These words are totally unhelpful and are a self-righteous denial of one's own sin. Yes these people have problems but they have a lot more in common with us than we like to think. They are people made in God's image although sinners like the rest of us and deserve proper diagnosis, treatment and care. Every effort needs to be made, if a violent component to their illness can be identified, to find a safe refuge for them until their illness is overcome.

Perhaps the laws governing mental health issues need to be changed when the possibility of violence towards others and self are present. I know it is complicated but surely in this age, we have the wisdom and knowledge to figure this out. "Our hands are tied" is not acceptable. If so, we need to "untie them". Since I have lived in Visalia, California for ten years, I know of two suicides, there no doubt were more, that have occurred within Reformed

This Poison Called Depression

churches. I know of way too many that have occurred with violence towards others as well.

The effects of depression in personal relationships are very destructive. For Betty and me there have been differences of understanding regarding the depressed person. She feels great compassion towards the depressed but also has a deep conviction that the depressed person can make changes, perhaps based on her observations of my dealing with depression. These changes, along with the proper use of medication and therapy, can help free himself from the depression and keep him out of depression. While I agree partially, my understanding places far greater importance on the biological component of depression and the proper treatment of it through medication. This has led us to misunderstand each other, argue, and even verbally fight with one another. Sometimes we have thought one of us simply refused to acknowledge the other's point of view or to take responsibility for his or her problem or to recognize the biological havoc that depression is making in the chemical composition of the brain. We have had our sleepless nights not because one of us is depressed but because we have gone to bed at night without being able to resolve our differences regarding what is happening to me and how that is affecting us. We have spent hours in silence for fear that what we might say will only widen the cavern between us. We have become angry because we see the other as stubborn and unwilling to alter his/her mindset or actions regarding depression. We have argued our cases, each of us finding articles and even books to support our assertions but the end result has been the same. We ended up hurting each other. We have needed to forgive each other and hold each other but sometimes that healing breakthrough has taken too long in its coming.

Lillian Grissen writes:
> Depression can be ascribed to either psychological or biological causes and often to both. Sometimes it is difficult to tell which precipitates what. Some researchers say that when there is a biochemical change in the brain, depression can result. Others say that depression seems to create the chemical imbalance. Each feeds the other and the sick person becomes sicker. Research on both causes is continuing. To operate normally, the brain requires a certain number of neurotransmitters which are chemical substances that transmit nerve impulses. When the brain is deficient in two of these chemicals, norepinephrine and serotonin, depression occurs. Research is demonstrating a shortage of neurotransmitters is something that can be inherited as it has in mine. (203)

It really is not surprising that Betty and I differ on this subject. The entire mental health system differs on it. Historically psychiatrists and psychologists have speculated over the issue: what is chemically induced (internal) and what is situationally induced (external) when it comes to depression? Sometimes the tension is worded differently but the tension is still there. Dr. Hart

This Poison Called Depression

in his book *Counseling,* writes: "Again and again I have encountered resistance on the part of my psychological colleagues to appropriate medical treatment of some depressions. . . . A simple diagnostic pointer is that the more serious the depression is in the absence of a recent significant loss, the more likely it is that the cause is biological" (88–89). As far as I know, this matter has not been resolved. William Styron writes, "The intense and sometimes comically strident factionalism that exists in present day psychiatry—the schism between the believers in psychotherapy and the adherents of pharmacology—resembles the medical quarrels of the eighteenth century" (11). I have always felt the tension and can share the statements of some of my psychologists and psychiatrists to underline this ongoing difference. One well-respected psychiatrist, who would admit that he spoke this word to simplify a complex problem, said the following: "When you are depressed, talk-therapy does not work; when you are no longer depressed you no longer need talk-therapy." A psychologist, on the other hand, insisted "that anti-depressants only work to clear the mind and after the mind is cleared you still have to deal with your issues." There may be truth in both statements but the difference in emphasis is clearly present. I felt this difference in my hospitalization when I was in two different hospitals both of which claimed to treat depression from both sides of the problem. They did, but clearly did so with more than a little tension between the two. I think it can be confusing to the patient. I am very grateful that a recent book, *Ministry with Persons with Mental Illness and their*

Families, calls for a better way: "The purpose of this book is to develop an integrated and interrelated approach that honors the work of specialists in psychiatry, psychology, and theology. It presents this approach as a dialogue between the disciplines so that each in her or his might work in partnership and not at cross-purposes, as often has been the case in dealing with mentally ill people." (Albers et al 5). I hope this will be the wave of the future in caring for the mentally ill.

Betty and I would also argue about what I was capable of doing. When we came home from our Midwest vacation, Betty thought it was time to paint the house. At first I thought so too. I began to scrape the areas where there was peeling and even started some undercoating, but the further I traveled into my depression, the more my brain and body objected to this risky adventure. Just about everything feels risky when one is depressed. Betty could not understand why I would no longer continue painting; after all I had nearly painted my way through college and seminary and had always painted the houses we had lived in along the way. But I could not make myself do it. I had great fear that I would do something drastically wrong, such as tip a can of paint over on the patio cement, fall off the ladder (I actually was a bit shaky), or get paint all over the windows. No doubt these risky behaviors were greatly exaggerated in my mind. It was this way with everything I considered doing. Many of you who read this will say, "So what- big deal" but to the depressed this feels extremely troublesome if not dangerous. I felt terribly threatened when getting groceries, driving the car,

This Poison Called Depression

having people over for refreshments after church, serving refreshments at church, or going to other people's homes for social interaction. I did not want to do it; I hated it because I felt too exposed.

This misunderstanding also affects the extended family and friendships. My daughter during this last depression suggested rather forcefully, keep in mind that I may have exaggerated her words in my mind, that I was talking too much about my depression to Betty. She felt that her mother was taking a verbal beating from me by my constant haranguing about how I felt. So she told me: "Put a sock in it." She was no doubt right and meant no disrespect towards me with her statement. Her remarks were an attempt to make me aware of what I was doing with my excessive talking about my depression with Betty. I am thankful for that. At the same time she did not really understand as to what I was feeling. Her concern does underline the need that depressed people have to share their burden with people other than their married partner or immediate family only. This is easy to say but very difficult to do. The church community needs to be open to this verbal sharing as it ministers to the depressed in their midst. But this requires willingness on the part of the depressed to share their feelings with trusted persons and the willingness on the part of the care-giver to listen to what might seem as an illogically structured verbal diatribe once the depressed person starts opening up.

Another person, a friend, at times also felt that I was not making a strong enough effort to overcome the depression. She made the mistake of asking: how are

Larry E. Van Essen

you doing today? I said, "I'm frustrated because I'm not getting any better." She responded with: "do you know what is frustrating? Your friends are trying to help you but you do not seem to care," a conclusion often made by those who have not experienced clinical depression. Typical responses that people make, as Lillian Grissen points out, are these: "If she would only stop feeling sorry for herself, she should snap out of it. She should trust the Lord. She should count her blessings. She has everything; what more does she want?" (211). One person said to me: "Are you just being naughty by your refusal to carry out your responsibilities?" Notice the word "refusal." It implies choice and willfulness. An elder said to me that "I refused to preach any longer." I would have loved to preach normally, but when one is depressed, one is living abnormally. Another said: "You certainly are fortunate to have very understanding elders who are giving you time off to recover from your depression. Not every pastor or person holding down a job would receive such generosity." This implies that I a depressed person was receiving consideration beyond what other people receive. To which I have later felt, "Oh yeah?" How about the person with terminal cancer, heart disease, or substance abuse? Often generous amounts of time are given by the employer and community until the sick person either recovers or dies. Many jobs provide sick days. One overwhelmed teacher, suffering from depression, told me that the school board was giving her six months off but at a reduced hourly wage. Now when I am not depressed I look back, smile, and think "if you only knew what it was like. Try playing golf with both hands tied behind your back."

In *Ministry with Persons with Mental Illness and their Families,* Robert Albers in his introduction says, "Those who are mentally ill might be considered as the "modern-day lepers" who suffer from a socially "unsanctioned illness" and who continue to be misunderstood and mistreated by society and religion alike as a consequence." (2) I thank him for putting this reality once again before the public. I recall how one of my psychiatrists cautioned me about desiring to be admitted to a mental health clinic or hospital for treatment. Being a clergy person in the Christian Reformed Church in North America, such a record might have an adverse effect on my future ministry opportunities, he warned. One would think that a statement from one's psychiatrist and other mental health practitioners affirming the current mental health of such a person would be sufficient.

While the effects of depression can be weakening, debilitating, life threatening, and relationally harmful they can also be strengthening, life affirming, and relationally up-building.

In my depression I was uplifted by the thought that a sinner such as I, who was completely broken and worn down, could still hope in God. As the psalmist says in 42 verse 5: "Put your hope in God." While my self-image was shattered, I found comfort in the fact that the psalmist who also was downcast dared to believe that he and others like him could still hope in God. While I felt unforgiven, I could still draw comfort, no matter how illogical, from a passage like Mark 9:24: "I do believe; help me overcome my unbelief." And while the depression lingered on for many long weeks, I found great relief every night in saying as I settled into bed: "Father into your hands I commit my spirit." It didn't matter at such precious times if I was depressed and feeling downcast because I could throw myself into the arms of my heavenly Father. I cannot explain how I still had some faith in God even though I was almost gone, except for the fact that He was holding me.

My depression was also life-affirming in that each day that God gave me the grace to live assured me of God's design and determination to have me live. I began to realize that the words of Psalm 139:8 were literally true for me: "If I make my bed in the depths, you are there." This occurred at the beginning of my recovery. Then and now I look back on those days and I find great strength in the fact that "All the days ordained for me were written in your book before one of them came to be" (16).

Strange as it may sound my depression deepened my relationship with Betty, family, and church members but at considerable struggle and pain.

Betty and I had serious differences and could not always resolve them, yet we were able on most occasions to say, "You know, while we do not understand what is happening right now, and we do not know where this is going to lead—perhaps I will end up boxing groceries or applying for disability—but whatever happens we still have each other and we will find our way through this." Betty proved to be courageously strong and lifted me up often by her steady faith. She would say more than once: "You did not get into this overnight and you will not get out of this overnight, but you will get out." Wow! My heart could receive this good news even though it was almost impervious to any hopeful statement during this time. Our relationship has deepened and has grown in ways that would never have occurred unless we traveled this road of depression together. Betty's sleep cycle was completely disturbed. There were times she would rub my back until 2 or 3 in the morning and wake up at 5:30 when she would start crying on the floor. It was horrible for her, and I feel guilty for putting her through it. I do not recommend depression to build relationships.

Our relationships with other family members and church friends were also strengthened. To hear the elders at Crossroads Church say: "We do not want you to worry about your job at church right now. All we want you to focus upon is getting better" was so incredibly freeing and supportive that we will never be able to adequately express our thanks. We received assurances of prayer from people we would have never guessed would be praying for us.

My brother Howard called and said: "Your life will never be the same again." My sister Rose assured me in a dark hour that God had given me a special gift with people and a special kind of personality that could affirm others in their sorrow and reach out to the hurting and the lost. Things that I had forgotten. My sister Jo assured me that she was praying for us and so did many other relatives and friends. I doubt if these affirmations would have been made were it not for the fact that I was so very sick. I was hanging on by the thinnest of faith. My son-in-law, Casey, said that I needed to live so that Isaac, a boy they were in the process of foster-caring with a view to adoption, could someday meet his grandpa. Now he is seven and has a brother Ethan. We truly enjoy these two as well as our other ten grandchildren. Our neighbor lady across the street upon hearing that I was home from the hospital and out of my depression exclaimed: "Praise the Lord." This was from a woman who had not been in church for years. Where do you go with your joy and gratitude if you cannot go to God? We have a plaque on the wall that reads: "Peace is seeing the sunset and knowing who to thank." How true.

The effects of depression are deeply negative and cut through to the core of our being, but they are also deeply positive, forever cementing relationships with God, friends, and family that few other things could have done.

It has always amazed me that people often do not notice that the depressed person is struggling, even failing in their job. I have preached sermons while depressed and people have commented on how well I have preached and how helpful the sermon was. Inwardly I was thinking, "Can't you see that I'm feeling horrible?" I was fully aware of what I could do when healthy and what I was not capable of at this particular time. I needed to say how it was.

When my last depression in 2006-07 was not leaving me, I shared with our senior pastor that I was not capable of doing my pastoral work adequately. He was very understanding, and it was not until several months later

This Poison Called Depression

that we started to say, "Maybe we should look at the retirement option"—as I had mentioned earlier. We did. After several weeks of discussion with a couple of elders from the church, we agreed that retirement was the route to go. It meant that I was retiring at age 64, a couple of years early, and so a certain amount of money would be proportionally deducted permanently both from my social security and minister's pension. It meant that I had to accept the fact that while I had firmly believed I would remain in active ministry until I was 66 and would retire in my 40th year of ministry, it simply was not going to happen. I was deeply disappointed.

Depression can get you fired, retired or recovered. This is a tough judgment call. How long can the church wait for a Pastor to recover? Where can the Pastor go to receive help? For example, I recently learned about the ministry of Quiet Waters in Denver, a place where Christian leaders can go for counseling intensives. Something similar is available in Fresno, called Link Care Center. Perhaps there were alternatives available. When one is not thinking clearly, self-care and self-advocacy are not possible so one party to the question of what needs to be done and what is available is not even minimally engaged. Open communication among the church's leaders with the depressed person, brainstorming as to what can be done, using the resources from the denominational office, and an occasional conversation with the doctors will help those involved arrive at satisfactory answers. I still wonder if other alternatives to retirement were available but simply missed. The thought of retirement created fears that we

Larry E. Van Essen

might lose our house, on which we were still making payments, or that we might not be able to manage our lives financially. And what would we do about health insurance before I could receive Medicare? But we were amicably able to work these issues out and I retired from the ministry in December of 2007.

Soon after retirement, I was working by my daughter caring for flowers, plants, lawn, weeds, leaves, broken sprinkler heads, raking, blowing, edging, and . . . aching. I remember saying to my work partner, "What do you do about your aching back?" He quickly responded, "Yes, what do you do about it?" He was implying that there is very little one can do about it. Wonderfully by the summer of 2008 I was completely recovered. Only six months after my retirement! Also, after about a year, I was blessed with an additional part-time job working for The Christian Reformed World Relief Committee, now World Renew, as a donor relations person here in California. I have thoroughly enjoyed this job because it seems to capture the heart of Jesus' ministry with its emphasis on ministry to the whole person with words and deeds. When I was in the active parish ministry, it always bothered me that the deed side of the gospel was not being adequately done by me but with World Renew it always is. I have come to think that "deeds" in the community create the pathway to healthy church growth. It has also put me in contact with many wonderful Christians with a passion to help the poor living with disease, disasters, hunger, and social injustice. Help them, but not enable them or create dependence. It captures the teaching of Micah 6 verse 8: "He has showed you, O man, what is good. And what does the Lord require of you? To act justly and to love mercy and to walk humbly with your God." I have been given occasional opportunities to preach as well, for which I am deeply grateful.

Chapter 3 discussion questions

1. Do you think that some kinds of depression are genetic?

2. Why is it often ineffective to reason with or read scripture to depressed people?

3. What does Styron mean when he says: "Even those for whom any kind of therapy is a futile exercise can look forward to the eventual passing of the storm."?

4. Is there a definite timeline for major depression?

Chapter 4

The role of Scripture, prayer, worship and caregivers in the healing of depression

I think there are several ways in which caregivers can be helpful in serving the mentally ill, perhaps with all illness. But all of them require a good deal of sensitivity.

When I was depressed it was very difficult to receive spiritually through my reading of the Bible, personal prayer, or corporate worship. I remember several incidences of people visiting and wanting to read from the Bible. Sometimes I was tired and did not want to hear anything more that I needed to think about. I felt like I had to tell the brother or sister, "Could we please do this some other time. I need to rest right now." One needs to be sensitive to the person whom he is visiting. Ask her if she would like you to read a passage from Scripture. Prayer, on the other hand, is always welcome. This may not be true for everyone, but it was true for me.

I also found that going to church, even though it was uncomfortable to be seen by people to whom I wanted or "ought" to be ministering, gave hope. I believed that congregational prayers that included general prayers of healing, if not specific prayers, might be answered and that the process of taking my need to God through the worship leader was comforting and encouraging. It gave me a sense of doing something about it. I would encourage depressed persons to rely firmly on the "communion of the saints" that we confess as part of our faith. I found it to be deeply true. I have no doubt that prayer and public worship played a huge role in my recovery, along with medication. I have observed that many people when ailing will back away from public worship, perhaps thinking they will not receive anything beneficial or perhaps worrying about how they may look physically, or what others might think. On balance I received encouragement and strength from corporate worship, even though I was not able to put myself into it. It was not magic, I am sure, but it did testify to the power and presence of the Holy Spirit when people were gathered in Jesus' name. My belief in healing is simple reformed, biblical, traditional faith. We should not underestimate this power nor shy away from it. Our faith has miraculous power! Shouting and screaming is not necessary. God hears, God understands and God heals.

One day when I had been in major depression for some time, a minister friend phoned. After introducing himself, he asked, "May I read from Isaiah 61:1–3 for you? I simply want you to hear this positive message." I said, "Please do." He read:

This Poison Called Depression

> The Spirit of the Sovereign Lord is on me, because the Lord has anointed me to preach good news to the poor.
> He has sent me to bind up the brokenhearted, to proclaim freedom for the captives and release from darkness for the prisoners,
>> to proclaim the year of the Lord's favor and the day of vengeance of our God,
>> to comfort all who mourn, and provide for those who grieve in Zion—
>> to bestow on them a crown of beauty instead of ashes, the oil of gladness instead of mourning, and a garment of praise instead of despair. . . .

Then he closed with a brief prayer that God would make this a reality in my life. I was blessed that day. I thanked him for calling. Please do not get the impression from the above that I am diminishing the power of God's Word. I think it is very powerful, but it needs to be handled wisely when ministering to the sick.

Occasional reminders that the writers of Psalms and other writers in the Bible spoke to God about their depression also encouraged me: Psalm 22, 23, 25, 30, 31, 32, 40, 42, 43, 46, 55, 62, 69, 71 and many more. Psalm 69:1-3 is especially descriptive- "Save me, O God, for the waters have come up to my neck. I sink in the miry depths, where there is no foothold. I have come into the deep waters; the floods engulf me, I am worn out calling for help; my throat is parched. My eyes fail, looking for God." Moses sounds depressed in Numbers 11:10–15,

Larry E. Van Essen

Job in Job 3, Jonah in Jonah chapters 2 and 4, Saul in 1 Samuel 16:14, 23, Elijah in 1 Kings 19, and Jesus in Matthew 26:37–46. Knowing that some of the spiritual giants in the Bible experienced depression gave me hope.

Reminders that other fellow human beings, outside of scripture, had struggled with depression and were able either to successfully cope with it or recover from it helped me. Abraham Lincoln, Winston Churchill, Charles Spurgeon, John Calvin, Martin Luther, Emily Dickinson, Gerard Manley Hopkins, Nathaniel Hawthorne, Fyodor Dostoevsky, J. S. Bach, and Ludwig von Beethoven were cited as being depressed at times.

I must add something about the Lord's Supper that may sound as if I have a Roman Catholic view of actually physically receiving the body and blood of Christ in eating and drinking the elements. I would rather think of it as actually spiritually receiving the body and blood of Christ. The act of eating and drinking, and hearing "This is my body and this is my blood" persuaded me that I was somehow taking in God's love, forgiveness, healing, and peace and relying on Christ to work in my life not only for my salvation but also for my recovery. This was powerful medicine.

In short, if you wish to serve the sick and especially the depressed, keep on ministering with the Word, prayer, and the Lord's Supper, remaining sensitive to the receiver, for "Where two or three come together in my name, there am I with them" (Matthew 18: 20).

An additional ministry that the church can provide those who are mentally ill and their families is to provide

This Poison Called Depression

accurate information on depression by offering books in the library, brochures on the literature counter, and occasional seminars on mental illness. There is no substitute for accurate information in ministering to the depressed. Archibald Hart says: "An accurate understanding of the nature and causes of depression is essential to helping someone who is depressed" (139).

The authors and editors of *Ministry With Persons with Mental Illness and Their Families,* affirm that "It is essential for caregivers to understand depression, not only because it is so common and potentially serious, but also because clergy and lay caregivers are likely to be the first people sought out by depressed parishioners or their families" (11). They also embrace the value of listening. "Listen! Listen! Listen! Listen with compassion, empathy, and patience, providing a ministry of a caring presence" (26). Your supportive presence with the depressed may be your most valuable contribution to the depressed person.

What an open door for Christians and the church this whole area of mental illness is. We carry on in the tradition of our founder Jesus. He summarized his ministry in saying, "The Spirit of the Lord is on me, because he has anointed me to preach good news to the poor. He has sent me to proclaim freedom for the prisoners and recovery of sight to the blind, and to release the oppressed." Christian caregivers can play a significant healing role in the life of persons and families with mental illness.

A contribution that Christians can and must make is advocacy for the marginalized. Many scriptures speak to this mandate such as: Micah 6:8, Matthew 4: 24,

14:14, 35-36. On the National Alliance on Mental Illness web. site (www.nami.org), a very important fact is cited concerning the high costs of cutting mental health care: "Mental health treatment works and is an investment in recovery. From models that support individuals with the most severe or complex conditions to treatments that provide relief for more moderate mental illness, mental health treatment saves lives and reduces other costs." Right now as we are struggling with our high national and state budgets and our huge deficits it is important that we all watch carefully as to what is being cut from mental health and programs that help the poor.

Chapter 4 discussion questions

1. Why is it so important when visiting sick people that caregivers of any kind remain sensitive to the patient? Does the sick person's condition take precedence over the caregiver's agenda?

2. Have you ever found public worship to be emotionally and spiritually helpful even though you could not enter into the worship experience?

3. Does it surprise you that Bible characters spoke about being depressed?

4. Do you think the church has an open door to ministry when it comes to mental illness? In what practical ways can you really help?

Chapter 5

The role of medication in the treatment of major depression

I had a difficult time at first accepting the fact that I needed medication to deal with the symptoms of my anxiety and depression. Many Christians do, saying or thinking, "If I have sufficient faith I should be able to overcome this! If we prayed hard enough, repented of all known sins in our life, we should be able to overcome this with God's help." When one reads the Scriptures, it implies or seems to imply that a person is responsible for cooperating with God in his/her own spiritual health. One needs only to hear Galatians 5:22, "But the fruit of the Spirit is love, joy, peace, patience, kindness, goodness, faithfulness, gentleness and self-control"; or 2 Peter 3:18, "grow in the grace and knowledge of our Lord and Savior Jesus Christ"; or Philippians 4:4, "Rejoice in the Lord always. I will say it again: Rejoice," to be convicted that living with passivity, sadness, ill feelings towards others, and lack of enthusiasm for kingdom activity cannot be glorifying God. When you are stuck in negative emotions, thoughts and spiritual habits, you can only conclude that something is definitely wrong with you and your relationship with God. And we with our Christian work ethic and values think that if something is wrong with us we ought to be about the task of fixing it. So in an effort to fix it, I tried self-help things such as exercise, thinking positively, focusing on other things beside the depression, listening to music, singing, counting my blessings, and reducing my schedule. All had been suggested to me. I may be forgetting some. But none of them by themselves or together worked for me.

My psychiatrists would always tell me that major depression is a chemical imbalance in the brain. Something was not working properly in the brain and if that was true then medicine to correct the problem undoubtedly was appropriate. The problem was not spiritual (lack of faith, disobedience to God, sins of commission or omission) or emotional but physical. Yes, a physical illness within the brain for which the proper treatment, at this point in time, is medication. This last sentence is the one I most want to be accepted by everyone in understanding major depression. I struggled long and hard before I could finally accept that it was indeed appropriate for a Christian to take medication for major depression. I had to untangle depression as illness from depression as my personal sin, weakness, or ineffective stress or anger management. Today I accept this fact and freely suggest to others who have major depression to follow their doctor's advice. As

Meller and Albers say, "Exactly why brain areas develop abnormalities and exactly how these abnormalities interact remain a mystery, but researchers continue to progress in understanding brain function" (17). Although Jamison was commenting on the treatment of manic-depressive illness, what she says holds true for those with major depression. "The major clinical problem in treating manic-depressive illness is not that there are not effective medications-there are-but that patients so often refuse to take them. Worse yet, because of a lack of information, poor medical advice, stigma, or fear of personal and professional reprisals, they do not seek treatment" (Jamison 6).

Chapter 5 discussion questions

1. If you ever became clinically depressed would you take medication? Why or why not?

2. If we are responsible for cooperating with God in our spiritual health than does not depression indicate our failure to do so?

3. Do you agree with the author when he says: "if that (depression being a chemical imbalance in the brain) is true than medicine undoubtedly is appropriate?" Why or why not?

4. Do you think that depressed people often refuse to take their medication and that because of lack of information, poor medical advice, stigma, or fear of personal and professional reprisals they do not seek treatment?

Chapter 6

The role of a therapist in the treatment of major depression

When you are facing such a devastating disease as major depression, it is essential that you find a professional therapist. I would suggest that you see both a psychologist, certified counselor and a psychiatrist who can prescribe the appropriate medication. Perhaps receiving both kinds of help is the best route to recovery. My life has been blest with wonderful counselors from both sides of the issue. Look around. Google the doctors and counselors in your city or county. Check with mental health organizations such as: National Alliance for the Mentally Ill (NAMI), National Alliance for Research on Schizophrenia and Depression (NARSAD), National Depressive and Manic-Depressive Association (NDMDA), National Institute of Mental Health (NIMH). The single worst mistake we make is waiting too long. John H. Timmerman writes the following about his journey with his wife, Pat, through depression:

> It was this biological depression that sucked my wife—and my family—into its black paw. We became a vivid example of suffering in the Christian life. . . . The first lesson our family learned from our experience was that people wait too long before seeking professional help for depression. (214)

As Deb Niehof wrote in a newsletter from Classis North Central Iowa of the Christian Reformed Church: "The good news is that there is help available. The last decade has seen an explosion of research and new medications for these diseases of the brain."

I do want to caution you about who you go to or what program you may try to do on your own. Some counselors simply do not believe in medication for depression and would not refer you to a psychiatrist. They prefer to use talk therapy exclusively. This means your treatment will be ineffective if your depression is a chemistry issue in your brain.

I have a particular program of CD's that is nicely packaged, but it says some rather outrageous things. For example, it questions whether major depression and anxiety is a mental illness, causing me to question whether its authors ever experienced or studied anxiety and depression in depth. They want me to believe that "recent studies show that cognitive behavioral skills are more effective than medication." The scary thing is that this particular program, according to its literature, is used by schools, the YMCA, Ford, McDonalds, and Chrysler. Hopefully this is merely typical advertisement exaggeration.

When you have an illness that causes you to live not at the bottom of the sea but beneath the bottom, you need to exercise caution when looking for help.

Chapter 6 discussion questions

1. Why does the author suggest that a depressed person seek help from both a psychiatrist and psychologist?

2. Why should a person use some caution when seeking help for major depression?

3. Do you think good professional help is available in the area where you live?

Chapter 7

The providence of God in depression

The providence of God is always a mystery, but I think it is especially so when dealing with depression. Now we are adding mystery to mystery. What good can come from something so indescribable, life threatening, and relationship challenging? For me it often came in the question, why would God allow this disease to inhabit my body for weeks and months at a time? Is God telling me that I really was never called to ministry and its time now to get out? Is God calling me to a certain kind of repentance that I cannot put my finger on? When God allows you to lay down the reigns of ministry for twelve weeks or allows you to face retirement from active parish ministry He is not fooling around. Or is this not God at all? Perhaps it is Satan? I choose to think that it is God allowing Satan to do this terrible work in me/ us.

I still have times, after four years of retirement from

Larry E. Van Essen

active parish ministry, that the questions come back, usually briefly. I have learned to accept the fact that God does not always answer our questions. Perhaps I should say, "Rarely does God answer our deepest question of why." Vance Havner says it well: "Whoever thinks he has the ways of God conveniently tabulated, analyzed, and correlated with convenient, glib answers to ease every question from aching hearts has not been far in this maze of mystery we call life" (66–67). Like Job in the Bible, we may come close to cursing the day of our birth (3:1), and we may have comforters who say seemingly right things:

> Your words have supported those who stumbled; you have strengthened faltering knees. But now trouble comes to you, and you are discouraged; it strikes you, and you are dismayed. Should not your piety be your confidence and your blameless ways your hope? (4:4–6)
> But if it were I, I would appeal to God; I would lay my cause before him. He performs wonders that cannot be fathomed, miracles that cannot be counted. (5:8–9)
>
> Blessed is the man whom God corrects; so do not despise the discipline of the Almighty. For he wounds, but he also binds up; he injures, but his hands also heal. (5:17–18).

But this does not mean that they are right or appropriate for the depressed person.

The book of Job is a dialogue between God and Job about the ways of God. The Lord does not speak

This Poison Called Depression

definitively until chapter 38. He does not answer Job's questions about his ways with him, but he gives Job a greater vision of who God is. "Where were you when I laid the earth's foundation? Tell me if you understand" (38:4). "What is the way to the place where the lightning is dispersed, or the place where the east winds are scattered over the earth?" (24). Finally Job responds:

> I know that you can do all things; no plan of yours can be thwarted. You asked who is this that obscures my counsel without knowledge. Surely I spoke of things I did not understand, things too wonderful for me to know. (42:2–3)

While the providence of God is a mystery to us, there was the reality that God was with me in my depression even though it did not feel that way to me. He was holding me in his arms. I and all who experience suffering of any kind, had/have to hold on to this reality strictly by faith. "Even though I walk through the valley of the shadow of death I will fear no evil for you are with me." (Psalms 23: 4)In my depression, I had to tell myself that God's word was still true even if my experience was strongly suggesting that it was not. Depression challenges one's faith. Reminders from others of this reality were desperately needed. It was as if I needed to live off and rely on the faith of others. Here too the Christian care-giver plays a very important role. The Bible's emphasis on God being with us in our good and bad times is very extensive. Consider Isaiah 43:2-5, Exodus 3:12, Joshua 1:5,9, Jeremiah 1:8, Judges

6:16, Matthew 28:19-20, 1: 23, John 14:17. Assurances of God being with us/me were a source of strength to me.

I believe that there is an additional aspect to our knowledge of God's ways. Not only is he with us in our suffering, he is also for us for our good. I know that Romans 8:28 can be used tritely, but it still conveys a profound truth that is itself a mystery. "And we know that in all things God works for the good of those who love him, who have been called according to his purpose." The idea of God working for the good of the believer in all things can be a strong anchor for the soul in the middle of suffering. Even though we may not feel it, see it, or understand it, it is still true. Joseph's words come to mind when he was so cruelly dealt with by his brothers. He is dumped into a well, mocked for his dreams, and sold to Midianites who bring him to Egypt where he eventually and remarkably becomes second in command over all of Egypt. Then his brothers come from their land to ask for food from him during a time of famine—it is a feel-good story but one also filled with rock-solid truth. Joseph exclaims:

> Do not be distressed and do not be angry with yourselves for selling me here, because it was to save lives that God sent me ahead of you. For two years now there has been famine in the land, and for the next five years there will not be plowing and reaping. But God sent me ahead of you to preserve for you a remnant on earth and to save your lives by a great deliverance. (Genesis 45:5–7)

This Poison Called Depression

Timothy Keller has insightfully commented on these verses in his book, *The Reason for God* (23ff). In a section entitled "Evil and Suffering isn't Evidence against God," he says the following:

> Tucked away within the assertion that the world is filled with pointless evil is a hidden premise, namely, that if evil appears pointless to me, then it must be pointless. This reasoning is, of course, fallacious. Just because you can't see or imagine a good reason why God might allow something to happen doesn't mean there can't be one. Again we see lurking within supposedly hard-nosed skepticism an enormous faith in one's own cognitive faculties. If our minds can't plumb the depths of the universe for good answers to suffering, well, then, there can't be any! This is blind faith of a high order. . . . If you have a God great and transcendent enough to be mad at because he hasn't stopped evil and suffering in the world, then you have (at the moment) a God great and transcendent enough to have good reasons for allowing it to continue that you can't know. Indeed, you can't have it both ways.

Keller goes on to cite Alvin Plantinga,
> a (secular) way of looking at the world has no place for genuine moral obligation of any sort . . . and thus no way to say there is such a thing as genuine and appalling wickedness. Accordingly,

> if you think there really is such a thing as horrifying wickedness [. . . and not just an illusion of some sort], then you have a powerful . . . argument [for the reality of God].

As I reflect back on my depressions, and ask: "what has God worked in me through my depressions?" What is the "for good" side? Several things come to mind.

I have received greater compassion for people in general and a desire to do what I can to help those who suffer.

I have gained a greater compassion for the poor. My depression has taught me that there are human conditions from which a person cannot free himself. We Christians freely admit this about our salvation from sin through Jesus Christ as a gift from God but it is true of other things as well. Try as I may I could not get better. Help was needed from others. Certainly poor people who are working but still cannot pay all their bills, even with the government aid that is available, do not need my criticism or judgment. I understand better than before that poverty like depression is complex and does not yield to simple solutions. Providing a meal is good. But more is needed. Training for jobs, good education, loving homes, health care, and much more is necessary. We need to also recognize that poor people have much to offer the world and I want to support them in reducing their problems as they use their resources in solving their problems.

I have received greater compassion and understanding for the mentally ill. I have received phone calls or had conversations with people looking for help. Often the question they have is

This Poison Called Depression

"how can I care for my brother, daughter, husband or some other relative who is depressed? I'm out of ideas and capacity to give care." Generally I say: "you have been doing a great job of caring for your loved one. I know because else you would not have called me. I generally add: "you cannot fix it." If your relative is receiving treatment with medication and or treatment through psychology or both, the best thing you can do is be available to them for whatever they might need. Listening, patience and spiritual support are invaluable to the depressed.

Because of this growing compassion for the mentally ill I want to be an advocate for them. I want to help remove the stigma of mental illness from the world and especially out of the church. I also want their health insurance to cover their mental illness as well as it covers other illness.

As I see it God would not permit this depression in my life for nothing. I believe that He wants me to use these experiences to help others. I believe God wants me to do what the Apostle Paul says in 2 Corinthians 1: 3-4 "Praise be to the God and Father of our Lord Jesus Christ, the Father of compassion and God of all comfort, who comforts us in all our troubles, so that we can comfort those in any trouble with the comfort we ourselves received from God."

As I look back over my life, one verse pops up in my mind: "He has rescued us [me] from the dominion of darkness and brought us into the kingdom of the Son he loves, in whom we have redemption, the forgiveness of sins" (Colossians 1:13–14).

Chapter 7 discussion questions

1. Is the providence of God always a mystery? What about Luke 13:1-5?

2. How does the book of Job, Romans 8:28 help us in understanding the Providence of God? Does the Lord answer Job's questions?

3. How can we hold on to the promise of God being with us in our adversity? How can fellow Christians help in this regard?

4. The Bible says that God is for us in our adversity. How does this help us understand that our suffering is purposeful?

5. The author suggests several "for good" results from his depression. Do you think such thinking is right?

6. How does 2 Corinthians 1:3-4 speak to our adversity?

Chapter 8

Relapses

My experience with depression tells me that it can return at any time. I wish I could say that once I recovered from an episode, I remained healthy until today. But it did not work that way.

Sometime in February of 2007, I began to notice that something was wrong again. I feared that depression had returned. I debated whether I should talk to my psychiatrist about this because I thought he might raise the dosage of or change the medications that I had been taking. I always take medication for depression now whether I am depressed or not. My doctor has explained to me that I will always be on medication to prevent it from returning. "In your case when it returns, it returns with a vengeance." I really did not want to experiment once again, over a period of a couple of months, to find out what might get me back on track. Finally I realized I had no choice. So, back I went to the psychiatrist to explain that I was having symptoms of depression.

I was right. My doctor increased the dosage and added another. In early summer, I felt completely overwhelmed by my work. As described in the last chapter, I had to accept the fact that I would not make the 40 years of ministry goal. If nothing else could be found, I needed to retire. Nothing else was found.

I was completely recovered by June of 2008. Was it the medication, different work outside with all of its manual demands, the support of my family and friends, or the prayers of God's people that made for recovery? I think it was the medication, therapy, prayers, support of family and friends mainly and different work partially. Whatever it was, God certainly was in the mix the whole way. He will be there for you as well.

Relapses discussion questions

1. Should a person who has had major depression think that it could return again?

2. What were the spiritual healers for the author and what were the physical healers?

Epilogue

Today as I write these words I feel great but I know that depression could return at any time. Most days I do not live in fear but in the courage that comes from the powerful Word of God(The Bible), the completed work of Jesus Christ for our forgiveness, the ongoing work of his recovery and hope for our brokenness, his indwelling Holy Spirit and his support through fellow Christians. These are our spiritual healers. There is also the assurance that modern medicine is continuing to understand more about major depression and recovery from it. Should you be struggling with major depression, I would encourage you to patiently trust in and accept the God who gave us his Son for our forgiveness and maturation into Christ, and the Holy Spirit who inspires us with faith, hope and love and so much more. Place your trust in him. I would also encourage you to use the help that modern psychology and psychiatry offers you knowing that these too are gifts from God.

Finally, as a Christian, you are in the strong and loving arms of God.

"For I am convinced that neither death nor life, neither angels nor demons, neither the present nor the future, nor any powers, neither height nor depth, nor anything else in all creation, will be able to separate us [me/you] from the love of God that is in Christ Jesus our Lord." (Romans 8:38–39)

Epilogue discussion questions

1. What are suggested by the author as possible things to do should you be dealing with major depression right now?

2. Is there hope? See Romans 8:38-39.

December 2012

About the Author

Larry E. Van Essen is a retired pastor of thirty eight years serving four churches in California, Colorado, and Wisconsin. He is the husband of Betty, father of three daughters and grandfather of twelve. He is a graduate of Dordt College Sioux Center, Iowa and Calvin Theological Seminary, Grand Rapids, Michigan. Now he works for *World Renew,* a Christian global community development and relief agency. He resides with his wife Betty in Visalia, California.

Bibliography

Albers, Albert H., Meller, William H, and Thurber, Steven D.,editors, *Ministry with Persons with Mental Illness and their families,* Copyright 2012 Fortress Press, Minneapolis.

Blazer, Dan G., Professor of Psychiatry and Behavioral Sciences at Duke University, in *Christianity Today*, March 2009.

Grissen, Lillian, V., *A Path Through the Sea*, William B. Eerdmans Publishing Company, Grand Rapids, Michigan. Copyright 1993.

Hart, Archibald, *Counseling the Depressed,* Resources for Christian Counseling, General Editor, Gary R. Collins, Word Publishing Dallas. Copyright 1987 by Word Incorporated.

Hart, Archibald, *Dark Clouds; Silver Linings,* published by Focus on the Family Publishing, copyright 1993.

Jamison Redman Kay, *An Unquiet Mind*. Published by Vintage Books, a division of Random House, Inc. Copyright 1995 by Kay Redfield Jamison.

Keller, Timothy, *The Reason for God*, published by the Penguin Group, copyright 2008 by Timothy Keller.

Plantinga, Cornelius,Jr. *A Sure Thing*. Published by CRC Publications, copyright 1986.

Rosenfeld, Isadore, *Parade Magazine,* September 19, 1999.

Scheller, Christine A, quoting Kay Redfield Jamison, John Hopkins University Professor of Psychiatry in *Christianity Today.*

Styron, William, *Darkness Visible,* Vintage House, A Division of Random House,INC., New York, copyright 1990.

Timmerman, John. The Christian Century, March 2, 1988.

Made in the USA
Lexington, KY
19 November 2013